To Ana:
For your encouragement and inspiration.

FOREWORD
BY
ROSANNA LEY

I'm delighted and honoured that I have been asked to write a foreword for the collection of poetry that follows.

I first met the author when he joined a writing group I was tutoring at Northbrook College, Worthing in 2007. I was immediately struck by his determination to succeed and by his passion for writing. Since that time, KD Langford has written short stories, scripts, feature articles and now poetry – and those qualities I first recognized still burn within him just as fiercely as they did eleven years ago.

KD Langford first began writing poetry in 2017 at a summer writing holiday I have been running for eight years at Finca el Cerrillo in Andalusia, Spain. It is a very special place which provides both tranquillity and inspiration for the writers who go there.

For KD Langford, poetic inspiration arrived in a torrent of words and images and he was prolific. In days he had written a number of poems, some of which have made it into this collection. Since then, he has undertaken more work on these early poems and has written many more, some inspired by writing exercises we have done at the Finca, which have acted as a springboard for ideas and subjects for more poems. Some of his personal experiences are also here in poems which are sometimes stark, often revealing pain and always
honest.

I myself find KD Langford's poetry very emotive; other writers too have been much moved by the emotion and poignancy contained in some of these poems. The subjects are varied – hopefully there is something for everyone and readers will relate to many of the issues, themes and feelings described. I hope you will agree with me when I say that these poems are special because they truly come from the heart.

Rosanna Ley 2018

COPYRIGHT

BIO

My name isn't KD Langford, KD Langford is the alias I have used for a little over ten years. I never have liked, wanted or enjoyed being the centre of attention, which is perhaps why I write under an alias? In my early days of writing, I wrote because I enjoyed it, never thinking for a moment of doing it as a career choice.

As a child, my teachers encouraged me to write more than what I had already done, and so I did just that—spending my lunch hour at secondary school inside the I.T room staring at the big box like monitors that were the norm in the late 80s early 90s. Interword was my choice of word processor, it was simple, and so I just wrote. I wrote about anything that came into my mind. My first story, Greyhall, was about me as a secret KGB agent living in a large country house on the banks or was it an island of Lake Windermere? The Lake District was a place I spent much of my childhood, going to see family members and staying in a white stone cottage for weekends with my side-kick at the time a fabulous dog called 'Lady.'

My writing changed after I moved to Worthing, a town on the coast outside of Brighton. It was a place that would be my home for six fabulous years of my life. I attended a creative writing class on Monday evenings for three years, and this class led to a string of creative writing holidays that I still go on to this day in sunny Spain. My writing from 2007, when I began the writing class changed, and I started this long journey to being an author.

One of my most significant issues, however, was the number of ideas that would come into my head and then other stories or ideas I would be working on were pushed to one side. It was like having a new toy. I didn't want to play with the old toy anymore. I wanted the new one instead! LOL!

In 2017, I tried my hand at writing poetry, and after meeting someone special who encouraged me, I found myself writing poems. It was a way to express myself in many ways, both good and bad. I lost my mum in 2013, the family life had become strained, and so writing for me was a way to avoid doing something silly. I was able to express myself about how I felt about the special someone in my life and the frustrations I had of others closer to home.

What 2020 and beyond has in store for me? Who knows, but if you'd like to join me, you'd be welcome on board.

CONTENTS

Alone I am in this world of life.

Alone I awake.

Alone are the rooms I wander through.

Alone are breaths I take.

Alone are the seconds of this day.

Alone I move through the day.

Alone I go to bed.

Alone is the hand that strokes your pillow.

Alone in the darkness I fall asleep.

Alone I wake to a dream.

Alone am I no longer as you take my hand.

Alone...

Love is light within the shadows of darkness and pain.

Love is fire, our burning desire.

Love is air, life itself.

Love is earth, the journey of hope.

Love is water, the carrier of dreams.

Love is cruel, shattering hearts.

Love is all.

He appears from the doorway hearing the sound of familiar voices carried on the summer breeze.

A smile of delight drifts across his face. Her hand lifts as their eyes meet.

He takes her soft hand.

Her grip is firm, confident, meaningful.

Her lips speak her name, the sound fades drowning to a pounding heart.

That day I wake to the annoying sound of the alarm ringing in my ear.

Cursing you as I do.

I drag myself out from the warmth of the bed.

Coldness clings to the walls; its arms reach out to sting the naked skin.

I drag myself to the bathroom.

I run my hand across the jagged radiator.

Shoulders deepen as the sharp, cold metal adds to the bitterness of the morning's blues.

Yesterday's smile has gone down under.

The belly rumbles.

Clockwise the shower dial turns.

Water falls in a torrid storm dancing upon my hand.

Where are you? I wonder as I wait for you to arrive.

But like the bus of yesterday, you don't arrive.

I push your buttons, turn your knobs and fight you.

But for now, you have won.

The smell of sweat shall cling to this body for today at least.

Perhaps tomorrow you will lose the battle.

The kettle boils.

Beans parade round and around as the lights shine down, warming up, and I watch the show.

Like a rocket, you launch into the air - a bid to escape your destiny only to come crashing back down to your final resting place.

I smother you with butter I do as the show comes to an end with around of beeps.

Steam curls into the air as I pour the main event over the drenched toast.

Through the open door, I watch as you arrive.

Like unwanted rain, you fall on the darkest day of the week and each other day.

A strip of lightning shoots across the darkened sky as you remind me why I hate this day.

This day called Monday.

A young woman.

Did walk along the seafront.

Wrapped up warm for the damp December morning.

Leapt into a puddle, a smile upon her face.

'Splash' she called.

The puddle took quite a liking to her and devoured her.

Her arms waved.

As she vanished without a trace.

Here I sit... In the shadows of another.

Here I sit. Waves lapping against my feet

Here I sit. The sun bearing down upon me.

Here I sit. Home to so many.

Here I sit. Waiting for you to return home those who I nurtured and those who I adopted, all are one.

Here I sit. Changing through the ages.

Here I wait. Hoping you'll come home.

Here I cry. An old life fading into the mists of time.

Here I celebrate. The joy of a newborn.

Here I sit. An English town called Worthing.

I message you.

I wait for you.

I see you online.

Why is there no reply?

I hate it when you don't reply.

I hate not having patience.

I hate you for being miles away.

I hate my heart longing for you.

I hate my mind being fixed on you.

I hate you being with someone else.

I hate the fact you changed my life.

I love to hate you.

I love you because you drive me crazy.

I love you because you are you.

I love you for making me a better person.

I love you because you complete me.

I love you because I just do.

I look to the stars.

Wondering who you are.

A smile appears pushing away today's fears.

I hold the pillow close as darkness hides this night.

I feel your arms around me.

I turn seeing your smile.

I feel the soft touch of your lips upon my cheek.

People pass us by pulling their cases on their way to their flight.

The words that you speak, drowned by the pounding of my heart.

I follow you as we near a gate, a plane waits to whisk us away.

The world fades away in a mixture of colour and sounds.

I sit by your side on the plane.

You take my hand, squeezing gently as our eyes meet.

I wonder where we're going.

I don't care.

I'm with you.

A mist drifts down.

I panic, unable to let go of your hand.

You're happy, I'm happy.

I don't want this to end.

"Don't go", I call from within.

The sky is blue, cloudless.

Birds sing in the distance.

The wind whistles through the empty streets.

Ageing buildings surround me from a time long past.

You stand on the steps that lead to the church of my heart.

I lift the camera...

I squeeze the button waking to a cold, dark, lonely room.

A smile upon my face and warm heart as I think of you this morning.

Gone is the blue sky from the morning.

Gone are birds chirping on the breeze.

Gone is the life from the trees that bristle in the wind.

Gone is joy amongst us men as we hunker down behind the mounds of dark earth.

Whistles of shells whirling through the afternoon sky.

Explosions of earth shatter this once peaceful place.

Trees fallen.

Trees lifeless.

Horses tremble amongst the hellish sounds of man's own destruction.

Like the Earth itself churned upside down as much as mankind.

Horses fall amongst the fallen comrades of man and boy.

The face of fear clings to those who arrive this day.

Stretches carried by weary souls off to collect their next fare.

Men prepare to dance with death once more this day to the sound of the devil's whistle.

Perhaps I will be luckier next time.

I look to the sky above clouds of smoke hiding the afternoon light from this day.

The pungent smell of death swells the senses.

Perhaps death is calling my name.

The rattle of machine gun fire echoes in the distance.

I pray holding the cross of the Lord that it shall be indeed my turn.

I ready myself watching as comrades race up the ladders as they walk gracefully towards the doors of death.

I pray I shall meet you again one day, in another place.

Perhaps a cup of tea, cakes or a jolly fine pint in the local pub.

For today at least I go to dance with death once more.

He sits alone.

A dim light shines on a picture of a smiling face frozen in time.

Shadows of the night cling to this darkened room tickled by the flames of a log burning fire that dance upon these walls.

They stand staring at him.

Some fuller, others fallen on their side, rolling across the table laughing at him.

A glass lies on the floor, red wine spilt like a pool of blood.

He sits slumped in his chair.

His head hangs in shame.

Enough to send him to sleep.

Gordon, Jack, Glen and Harvey watch from the table.

Their lives shortened by his loneliness.

Their price for his despair.

Time waits for no one or so they say.

Time waits for that special moment to come.

Time waits for no one when you're on that date you've waited weeks for.

Time drags out Monday to Friday.

Time speeds through the weekend though.

Time is a healer.

Time at times can be cruel.

Time lasts longer than you or I.

Time to say farewell for now.

Why must you lie to me?

Why must you lie to your own?

Cut from the same cloth you and I.

And yet you lie.

Each lie you speak.

Questions the heart that beats within you.

I ask you: are you proud of me?

You reply you are.

How hollow it seems.

That the wind would breeze and whistle through a now lifeless tree on a wintry day.

I question what you feel anything for me.

I offer you a hand and you turn away.

Carrying on along the road of despair.

Do you lie again I indeed do wonder as you talk about your nameless friends.

Friends you see every month,

Unable to name them when I ask about them

Instead looking down upon the spinning wheel at which you sit spinning another web of deceit.

Each lie you spin, another gust of wind in the sails of my life that pushes me away from you.

I wonder will there many breaths left inside you or will it be your last upon our final goodbye.

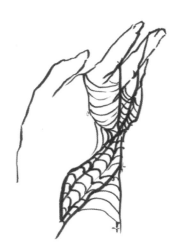

Cancer...

Cancer took you from my life.

A heart shattered, broken, beat without meaning.

Lost in life's wilderness.

On a journey out of control.

What was the point in continuing?

Life or death.

Only the latter seemed appealing.

Resentful had I become at those embarking upon that journey.

Unable to do the deed I'd longed for.

"What will I do without you?" were the words I spoke to you.

"Something will appear," you replied.

Time passed and she appeared before me.

A day turned into another day and another day after that.

A broken heart began to beat with meaning once again.

The seed of desire grew.

Branches grew and flourished

A new life had been born.

Back to this thing called life.

This heart beats strong, meaningful, space for only one.

The one who mended this broken heart.

Now beats calling out for you to come and for us to be one.

You are the beacon lightening up this darkened world.

Your ora of light shone brightly.

I lived in a world of darkness where the sun had long gone from this empty soul.

You brought hope.

You brought a new life to this lonely soul.

A gift that I longed for during the past years of walking through this world alone.

I feel you with this soul.

Lifting me up when I'm down.

You're the wind in my sails.

Pushing me on my way.

Even though we are not one, I see you in the dreams.

Through the seeds of life.

Dreams tendered growing into life itself.

I sit alone amongst the hills of Sierra Almijara to which
I call home.
Unloved I sat through the passing moons and the ris-
ing suns.
A heavy soul.
Home to a faded heart.
Lost and forgotten.

Two strangers from a distant land came.
Hope in their hearts.
A vision for their dreams they saw in me.
And so a new life began for this weary soul.

People near and far come to see me through the
ages.
Some to walk.
Others to capture a moment on a canvass.
A few to spin the strands of their imagination.
As the sun hides away and the moon appears.
Friends gather to laugh, play and chat about their
day.

For some, I am a place of hope.
For others, I am a place of friendship.
For a few, I am the seed of life.
For many, I am and have been home.
For my name is Finca el Cerrioll.

A question is a sentence that awaits an answer?

You might think the answer is correct, but how do you know?

Things happen to us that seem to make little sense at the time, and we ask a question.

Which leads to yet more questions about the ones we've previously asked.

When is it your final answer?

A question...

A question... Will be answered eventually, but when do you know it has been answered?

Can an answer be more than one?

A question is like life itself.

Why did you tell me to go there?

Why did I meet her?

Why did I go on holiday?

Why are you not out of my life?

Why did she come into my life?

Why will you not let go?

Why is life so confusing?

And will I ever get an answer to this question?

Like many things in life.

One thing is certain, Time will Tell...

Here, there and everything darkness does linger through this ghostly mist.

I flap my sails in frustration as the wind gently pushes me through this night that haunts thee.

Wave lap against me to the gentle tone of the ships bell that rings out.

Chills travel upon this night as the devil dances with the sailors.

Sending shivers travelling up and down their spines.

More Rum they do call as they sing sea shanties.

The horned one dances upon the wooden decks with much delight.

For this night belongs to he who taunts those who seek his treasure.

I give you my first because you stole my heart the moment these eyes fell upon you.

My second because one is such a lonely number.

I give you my third because I love you.

My fourth because you complete me.

I give you my fifth hoping one day you'll

give me your heart.

My sixth rose because I want to be yours.

Alone rose did open up upon this day many moons ago.

With each passing year, another rose opens to the world to celebrate the lives you touch both near and far from home.

Your eyes glow like a wood burning fire that crackles and sputters welcoming us home from the harshness of the world outside.

Your laughter lifts even the heaviest of hearts bringing a smile to those who's faces crack and crumble.

Your smile pulls us through dark days. Blowing away the clouds of fear, uncertainty and bringing light and joy to those who know you.

And so this year we have come to visit & to wish you a happy birthday.

Our journey is shorter and longer than others we meet.

Some sail ahead on the Ocean in this world.

Others sail behind on the horizon.

Some will be with you sailing side-by-side.

Others will sink to the bottom of your life.

An image now lost in the mist of a darkened December morning.

A few we remember, holding them close to us. A treasured image locked in a glass cabinet away from the rays of the life.

So not to fade that moment of life that will flick us by, as we prepare to say goodbye to this world for the next.

Life is indeed a wonderful thing.

My friend
For many years now we have been friends.
By my side, you have always been through the good times and the bad.
You have guided me through this thing called life.
Helped me when I have made bad decisions.
Helped me to my feet when I've fallen.
Supported me when I've been down.

My friend.
I thank you for all you have given me.
I thank you for being my friend.
I thank you for holding my hand through the hardest year of my life.
I thank you for preparing me for the saddest goodbye I've yet made in this world of mine.
For giving me the strength to continue on this thing called life.

My friend.
I thank you for being by my side and protecting me from the dangers that others would have been caught in.
For the best years of my life where I lived the good life and accomplished much.
For the people, you introduced me to.
The people who inspired me.
For those who I let go and for those who remain.
For introducing me to the special one. The one who beats inside my heart.

My friend.
I hope one day we shall meet.
I hope one day I shall see your face.
Know the name you go by.
For now my friend - I write this poem to say thank you.

As if only yesterday I do remember.
I remember the news you gave me those years ago.
I remember being told how this would end.
I tried to ignore it.

As if only yesterday I do remember.
I remember the moment you rose to your feet.
Approached me and gave me the news.
The news that it had returned and time was short.

I remember the drive I made to see you one final
time.
A closed door.
A light blue curtain drawn across the window pane.
Number 7 on the door.
I remember opening the door.
Stepping in and seeing you there.
I remember taking your hand. Your eyes opened look-
ing to the way in which you had ascended to that
place we shall be united one day.

I remember the church being full of people who you
had known. Who respected you.
No one more so than me.
Pain and sorrow weighed these shoulder down that
day.
Heaven cried for me that day.
I kissed you once more before waving one final good-
bye.

I remember people asking me how I managed after
you had passed.
I remember crying on my first birthday without you.
I remember wanting only a hug.
I remember you with each beat of this heart.

Roar of thunder echoes from above.

Tearing through the bright blue cloudless sky.

Dust swirls up in a violet rage.

Shades of darkness creep through.

People coughing drowning out their cries for help.

Allah Aka Bar someone calls.

As another young child is pulled from the rubble of their home

Cries calling out for a mother a language we all can tell.

Arms and legs lie still of a fallen Syrian soul.

A mother, father, cousin, brother or sister.

The pale face of a stranger to this war-torn land a red cross upon their helmet.

A battered Mercedes rumbles along the war-torn street stopping to carry the injured from the injustice of mankind's own self-destruction.

The grim reaper watches with glee. Counting the souls like a banker counting his coins.

Crackle of gunfire echoes in the distance

as another plane prepares to dive upon its prey.

Another house falls apart.

A child's teddy tumbles down across the rubble. A smile upon its face.

Sirens whale in the distance.

As the booming sound of war ripples through the historic streets of a city called Damascus.

Stole my heart, so you did

Tossed to the side, so you did.

Found it, so I did

Lying in a gutter

Cold and alone

Calling your name, so it did

Found another, so you did

Embraced it, so you did

Heaven cried for me that day when you said I do.

Home is where I was born.

Home is where I hold that first image on the journey of life.

Home is where I stumbled.

Home is where I felt the back of mum's hand.

Home is where I tasted love for the first time.

Home is where heaven sang that Tuesday morning.

Home is where I cried that August afternoon.

Home is wherever you are.

Your smile comes in many forms.

It's a caring arm around me.

It's a hand reaching out when I'm fallen.

It's the wind in my sails.

It's the spinner spinning another yarn of poetry deep from within.

It's a musician pulling the strings of this heart that plays your name each day.

Your smile whispers your words in my ear when I'm alone.

I turn to say Hello.

It's given but never returned.

Watched from down the street.

It travels on the breeze.

It beats each day.

It calls your name.

I watch.

I wait.

Shoulders heavy.

A southern smile.

Time to sell.

Time to move.

Move to a two-way street.

You roar to life.

Awaking from your sleep.

Sun shines down upon you this day.

The flames of fury push you on your way.

Faster and faster you race.

Into the sky, you soar.

Alone you dance through the morning sky.

Roar of thunder ripples through the streets below.

Announcing your presence.

Terror whales from beneath.

Side-to-side you do fly.

Hunting this morning's prey.

Splutter of fire irrupts from beneath.

You turn sharply and climb high into the sky.

For now, you are safe.

For the hunter, time is short.

The hunter becomes the hunted.

Prey within sight.

Rage and fury clash as they push you down.

Hell explodes behind you.

Leaving a trail of destruction

Rattle of fire as those who escape your grasp.

The whooshing sound of your rockets launched with no care.

Vengeance on your mind as you head off home.

Proud you live to fight another day.

Sadness you kill those you aim to protect.

Hope in your heart.

Hope you'll have a nice day.

Hope the bus will be on time.

The train won't be delayed.

You might even get a seat.

All we can do is hope.

Hope is a strange thing.

Hope the weather will be better today than it was yesterday.

Hope she'll actually notice me.

Does she actually think of me.

I hope so.

Hope I'll get the right numbers.

Hope I'll make it to the end of the day.

Hope I'm as lucky tomorrow as I am today.

Hope you liked it...

Heaven smiles upon this place.

Hiding in the blue the light of the night.

Bells of heaven ring out.

Crowds gather smiles upon their face.

Horses clatter as they draw near.

A gold leaf carriage appears.

An angel climbs from the carriage.

A smile of delight fills her face.

An image of you and I perhaps one day?

Dressed in snow she walks towards the church of another man's heart.

Stars explode as images of her special moment captured in time.

I raise a toast to her good health.

Wondering if it'll ever happen to me.

Wondering will you be the one.

Wondering if you'll ever see me again.

Wondering if I even care.

Then I look at your empty chair.

Then I know I care...

Darkest depths of this soul.

A storm builds this day.

Trees grip to the barren earth.

Leaves torn from their mother's arms.

Dark skies block the light of calmness of the day.

Seas dance in fury to the cracking whip of the lightning.

Thunder roars its hell building.

As I read the words of the mind.

The temper does indeed begin to calm with each passing moment.

The storm drifting away for another day.

A heart beat without meaning.

Drained by events of life.

Weighed down with doubt.

Fear hung round its neck.

A broken heart.

Hope stopped by one day.

Gradually, hope built a candle in this place.

A beacon of Hope.

Shrouds of darkness wilted away.

The flame flickered brightly lighting up this dark place.

Desire saw this bright light.

Hope and Desire became one.

Doubt packed its bags and disappeared over the hill.

Fear tried extinguishing the flame of Hope and Desire.

But got too close and burnt away.

Time passed and much could be seen.

New opportunities came knocking on this door.

Each beat calls your name.

The beats went unanswered.

Desire tired packed its bags and moved on.

As darkness moved in

The world not as bright as it had been.

Winds of change drew in from all around.

Hope indeed looked away.

But it too packed its bags and went on its way.

This candle still flickers in this darkened world.

Reaching out for new hope and new desires.

Banishing darkness from this life of mine.

Heavy are the days without you.

Heavy is the weight I carry on my shoulders

Heavy are the hours working for that time and place.

Heavy...

Heavy comes lighter as we grow to the weight we carry.

Lighter are the days I see you happy.

Lighter is the acceptance we're not meant to be.

Lighter are the coming days when things get easier.

Lighter is the mist that hides you from my heart.

Lighter comes with time.

Lighter is the next step up.

Lighter is the chance to give back.

Lighter is when you see light at the end of the tunnel.

Lighter is light.

On a Monday you're a distant memory.

On a Tuesday you appear on the mind.

On a Wednesday I start to think what we should do with you.

On a Thursday I begin to smile.

On a Friday I'm celebrating your back in my life.

On a Saturday I am free.

On a Sunday I am sad.

People talk.

People celebrate.

People hug you.

Others kiss you.

A lucky one is held in your heart as they hold you close as the moon sets.

Two hearts beating as one.

A strong heart beats far-far away pounding your name.

The winds whistle past.

Stars in your eyes shine brightly this night.

Two lovers walk hand-in-hand over a shingle beach.

For I shall make do with the darkness of a cloudy night.

I dance with you in my open arms.

A dream as the heavens cry for me tonight.

Wondering if you remember me too?

A faded image locked in my heart.

A smile I give you.

As well as something personal from me to you.

As I call from afar.

Happy Birthday.

Knock knock goes the door

Heart skips a beat

As I let you in capture my heart As you do

A lost sheep stars in your eyes

I follow your voice

Through the mists of this desire

I follow you

Fading into ibis as time walks by

I shut the door as you walk out.

Calling farewell my love

I wish you well.

You make me smile

You make me cry

You make me leap out of bed although you are not by myside.

You make me sad when I call your name and there's no reply.

You make me smile when I am alone.

You make the burdens of a bad day fly away.

You make me happy.

You make my heart skip a beat.

You make me think.

You make me weak.

You make me want no one else.

You make me complete.

A thousand moons have I looked upon.
A thousand suns have shone down upon me.
Winds of time have run through me like children play-
ing.
Fallen tears once danced upon my hat now dance
within thee.

People come near and far to see me.
Write about me having never been to see me.
Sing about me as they once sang from within thee.
Capture moments in my life, unlike others use too.

I look out across the North Sea.
Once I lived in Northumbria.
Now I am a Yorkshire Lass.
Where shall I be in a thousand years?

I am the resting place for many.
Carers.
Visitors.
Princesses.
Queens
Kings

I have been a Christian.
A Benedictine.
A monastery.
And now an Abbey.

Although I am not the Abbey, I once was.
I am still standing.
For I am Whitby Abbey

The pub is empty.

I sit at the usual place.

I stare out of the window watching people come and go.

I stare at the darkness of the magical Irish stout that sits before me.

A perfect figure of beauty.

Chills running down it's naked body.

Dry lips call out.

I lift the glass as the creamy head smoothers my lips as I take sip.

The chills sending a tingle of delight through me.

Like a cat who's just had the cream I lick my lips.

Resting the glass upon the table.

One turns to two, two to three.

A fourth one is not yet coming.

Strangers come in, finding a table whilst others crowd the bar.

Child play, out of sight, but not out of mind.

A baby cries out in a language only they can understand.

My ears listen for anything useful.

Rugby talk & last night fight is all that the ears pick up.

I take a sip of stout it tastes good shame about the conversation.

No more I swear to myself, but who am I to kid.

The ears pay no more attention deciding to fix their attention to the jukebox playing some old tune for a decade before I arrived.

Four becomes five.

I stare at the empty glasses.

A sixth one?

There shall be no more.

Greyness lingers beyond the window.

Tears from the gods, no doubt will be coming.

I stagger to my feet. Looks of displeasure from the elderly couple who sit close by.

I turn and smile once more as the mumble to themselves.

How luck am I feel that a couple of strangers have nothing better to talk about than myself.

The jolly fat barmaid wishes me well as I wave farewell.

Forgotten you are to the day before today.

Unknown you are to tomorrow.

Open your eyes.

Your heart.

Embrace this day known as today.

Once today has passed you by.

Forgotten you will be to this day called today.

I walk through the halls of life.

Paintings hang on the walls.

Portraits of those past and present.

I stand staring at your portrait in the hall of a stranger.

Wondering if it will ever hang pride of place in my hall of life.

You stand staring at me.

A moment captured in time.

Waves crash behind you against the rocks of desire.

The moon and stars shine brightly in your eyes.

Capturing my heart.

Drawing me into your arms.

Capturing my soul.

I watch from afar.

A heavy heart beats in this lonely body.

A tear swells up from this empty soul.

Night falls as you sail off into the sunset.

Certain our paths shall never meet upon the sea of this life.

Another time.

Another place.

Perhaps.

For now I shall say farewell.

Travelling faster than the speed of light.

Shooting Star...

I wish upon a Star...

Faster than the speed of light.

Faster I wonder will you hear my call.

Shooting Star is what you are.

Starry night I feel your presence.

Miles apart a Shooting Star will link us this night.

Shooting star, I wish upon you tonight.

Shooting star hear my call I plead tonight.

Shooting star bring her close to me.

Shooting Star that's what you are.

Falling star come to this night in the dream of mine.

You're a shooting star.

Lighting up this lifeless soul of mine.

I wish upon a falling star.

Wishing you'd be mine tonight.

Shooting Star that is what you are.

Walking here alone, without.

Thinking of the times we'd spend together.

Holding you in my arms I feel your presence in the heart that beat against your chest as we said our goodbyes.

Shooting Star is a dream so far.

Shooting Star bringing my dreams to this darkened world.

Remembering this town when it was so different.

Remembering it now without you here with me.

Shooting Star bringing me back my dreams.

Falling Star taking me down.

We're never far apart our hearts united as one.

Every beat I think of you.

Each breath calls your names.

Every moment without is like a dagger to the chest.

Perhaps we should be as one...

Fire flickers in the darkened room.

Your picture hangs above the burning flames.

Keeping the this lonely soul warm at night you meet me in my dreams.

Shooting Star...

I wished upon a star.

A star that never leaves this broken heart of mine.

Broken by your absence.

Broken by a foolish mistake...

Broken by words that never should have been spoken.

Like a Falling Star.

Shooting Star...

You used to fall through the letterbox.

I used to be able to escape your grasp although only for a period.

I bury my head in the sands of time where darkness lingers.

I couldn't see you.

I never heard you.

You didn't exist.

Now you are with me all the time.

You ring announcing your presence.

Is it a message from a friend, no it's you again?

Children play innocence still on their side. Unaware of what lingers over the hill.

I sip my cocktail by the pool.

I'll pay for the holiday when I get back.

The mound was once small.

I blank the image from my mind.

I love Sunday's.

The one day the postman doesn't work, and the mailbox is left untouched.

I know I will drown one day.

Whether it will be the water or you that gets me first.

The kids moan.

The flight is cancelled.

The wallet is empty.

The credit card, fat, tired and worn out like me.

Declined appears across the screen.

Declined again.

The wife groans then moans.

I nod as her words fall upon deaf ears.

Bills...

I hate bills.

Upon this day...

As you look upon yourself...

A voice whispers in your ear...

A voice of a caring soul...

Who's face you might know or might not know...

That choice is indeed yours...

The voice might be male or female...

But who I am to say...?

The voice is a caring soul...

For that I do indeed know...

And so...

This caring soul shall indeed be with you...

It's arm around you...

As it calls upon the winds of the north to blow away your fears...

Lightening from within shall strike shattering the shackles that weigh you down...

It'll cry for you until all your troubles are washed away and a smile is upon your face...

It'll walk with you at your side or behind you...

Until these bad days are a faded image lost in the mists of time...

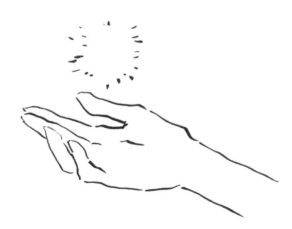

THE END

SOCIAL MEDIA

 @KDLANGFORD

 KDLANGFORD

Printed in Great Britain
by Amazon